Beauty in the Breakdown

May light be on you now
+ forever,

Renee Lynn Furlow

Renee Lynn Furlow

Edited by **Candice Daquin**
Formatting by **Ashley Jane Aesthetics**

Renee Lynn Furlow
USA

Author's Note: Pieces marked by a (*) throughout the book are pieces inspired by Mandy's Prompt Series. https://www.mandysteward.com/

BEAUTY IN THE BREAKDOWN/Renee Lynn Furlow 1st Edition
ISBN: 978-1-7372810-8-5

To the warriors who survive in spite of it all,
to those who have learned

there is beauty in the breakdown

Foreword

So, listen folks, you're in for a treat! What this down-home Texan girl knows about life is intertwined into a tapestry, a menagerie of journeys through a poet's heart and heartaches. And it is my honor and pleasure to call Renee Furlow my homegirl, even from Minne-snowta.

"I want to be a writer." Either you or someone that you know has uttered these words. Renee never had to wish or want because she's been a poet for almost as long as she can remember. Renee felt it in her bones and her passion moved her into publishing.

When our mutual friend introduced us, we knew immediately that we'd found a kindred spirit. Soon, we would become pen pals, sisters by choice, and besties. I've been impressed by her poetry and blessed by her words, in life and on the page, since day 1.

How do you encompass a woman who has so many demands in front of her and warrior wounds behind her, yet she continues to move along with grace, elegance, and a pen in hand? Renee's an empath, a poet, and a survivor. She's a gift and wonder. Whether you're new to Renee's work or an avid follower, please know that she's about to awe you with her prose. So proud to call Renee my friend and honored to introduce her book to you. May you be as touched and encouraged by her words as I've been.

With love and admiration,
Luann Miller

Playlist of My Poetry Writing

Numb - Linkin Park
The Catalyst - Linkin Park
Papercut - Linkin Park
Invisible - Linkin Park
Broken Pieces Shine - Evanescence
My Immortal - Evanescence
Lithium - Evanescence
Your Star - Evanescence
Lose Control - Evanescence
Imperfection - Evanescence
Right Beside You - Sophie B Hawkins
Did We Not Choose Each Other - Sophie B Hawkins
Heaven Don't Have A Name - Jeremy Renner
Sign - Jeremy Renner
Main Attraction - Jeremy Renner
Just My Type - Jeremy Renner
Just Tonight - The Pretty Reckless
Amaranth - Nightwish
Head Like A Hole - Nine Inch Nails
Down In It - Nine Inch Nails
Nightmare - Halsey
You - Candlebox
Pop - Nsync
Better Place - Nsync
Somebody That I Used To Know - Gotye
The Special Two - Missy Higgins
Outrunning - Ryan Jesse
Fading Like A Flower - Roxette
No Good For Me - The Corrs
The Wind - PJ Harvey
Possession - Sarah MacLachlan
Elsewhere - Sarah MacLachlan
Uninvited - Alanis Morissette
You Oughtta Know - Alanis Morissette
The Power of Goodbye - Madonna
Secret - Madonna
La Isla Bonita - Madonna

Live To Tell - Madonna
Angels - Within Temptation
All I Need - Within Temptation
Damaged - Plumb
Deliver Me - Sarah Brightman
Insensitive - Jann Arden
Gasoline - Jann Arden
Monster - Melissa Ethridge
I'm the Only One - Melissa Ethridge
Tonight and the Rest of My Life - Nina Gordon
Mirrors - Justin Timberlake
Do You Sleep? - Lisa Loeb
Sandalwood - Lisa Loeb
Headstrong - Trapt
Never Too Late - Three Days Grace
When I'm Gone - 3 Doors Down
It's Been Awhile - Staind
Outside - Staind
Who Is It? - Michael Jackson
Collide - Howie Day
She Says - Howie Day
Voodoo - Godsmack
Kiss the Rain - Billie Myers
Breathe (2AM) - Anna Nalick
Fast Car - Tracy Chapman
Therefore I Am - Billie Eilish
Cradle - The Rising
Gravity - Embassy
Savin' Me - Nickelback
Meet Virginia - Train
Drops of Jupiter - Train
This Is How A Hard Breaks - Rob Thomas
Unwell - Rob Thomas
Sick Cycle Carousel - Lifehouse
Desperately Wanting - Better Than Ezra
Breakdown - Tantric
Losing Grip - Avril Lavigne
Forgotten - Avril Lavigne
Tears of the Dragon - Bruce Dickinson
Just Like A Pill - Pink

Incomplete - Backstreet Boys
Untitled (How Could This Happen To Me?) - Simple Plan
Come Undone - Duran Duran
Break Me Shake Me - Savage Garden
Kiss From A Rose - Seal
Africa - Toto
Careless Whisper - George Michael
Alone - Heart
What Do I Have To Do? - Stabbing Westward
I Survived You - Clay Aiken
Bad Habits - Ed Sheeran
Because of You - Kelly Clarkson
Whataya Want From Me - Adam Lambert
Boulevard of Broken Dreams - Green Day
Somewhere Only We Know - Keane
Hunter - Dido
Save Tonight - Eagle Eye Cherry
What Hurts the Most - Rascal Flatts
Right Through You - Alanis Morissette
Smooth - Santana with Rob Thomas
Can't We Try - Dan Hill, Vonda Shepherd
What Do I Have To Do - Stabbing Westward
King Of Wishful Thinking - Go West
I Survived You - Clay Aiken

To Grow, You Must Outgrow

Completely losing control
is not something she's done often
But in her mind,
it feels like she lost control a few times

She replays times in her life
where different choices could have been made
which could have led to a completely different life

Regrets snake around every corner of her brain
Her mistakes seem to size her up and down
at every - single - turn

Inside
her dreams are realized
her ghosts hushed
her fears released
Taking time out to rest
had become the norm -
not even wanting to acknowledge
what frightening things
were awaiting her
on the other side

To **grow**...
you must **outgrow**

She feels she has outgrown
the cutout she has called home
for way too long

She has dreams waiting
on the other side of the fears
She has had the keys all along
to release herself from a prison

Time to unlock
Time to turn right side up

Finally,
she feels she doesn't have to
chase down those dreams
They have been in front of her
the whole time

Getting out of her own way,
she rose from the slumber
and decided it was time
to fully envelop herself
into the new reality

She was ready *to live*

Knowing

There's nothing
like the feeling
of knowing
the answers
are not out there

but
inside

where they've been
all along

See Around Me*

All I ask
is for you to see me
so clearly -

not see around me

Liminal Space

There is a quiet understanding
within the space between
each of the words
Finding the light
obviously became a beacon
for reaching the peak
The highest point reached
became a place of understanding
where those spaces
communicated
all that was needed to know

Reflective Truth

To see yourself as who you are
in your true essence,
all you have to do is look up

and see your reflection
in the stars

A Light in The Dark

Traveling down the many paths
of life and the choices I made,
I have learned
in all of these twists and turns,
in going under and over,
inside out and upside down,
finding the bright spots makes
such a difference
but also
ensures that you find
those darker trails as well
While the clear paths bring you light,
the darker routes offer something too -

They show you that **you** are
a light in the dark

A Spirit on Fire

Once the spirit is lit on fire,
changes are ushered in -
a breeze of pure clarity

Finding peace in small moments...
the heat begins retreating
Crisp air fills life
with a light tap on the back
and the reminder is HOLY

Transitions must take place
in each moment and season
Discovering new sides of oneself
is ultimately the reason

Choosing Silence

Holding her heart
more visible
than most,
she treats life as
a show and tell

Feelings validated
must be found
This led to her existing
as an open wound

Not every chapter
needed to be perfect

In reality,
true acceptance
is found within

And others
will admire her
for the times
she chose **silence**

Memory of Forgiveness

Taking place under the same sky,
a defensive edge unexpectedly sharp,
yellow lights of caution causing reactions
within familiar souls
Signs of stress come in fours,
incomplete thoughts searching for a point
within months of discarded dollars
This internal struggle will
soon
soon
be forgiven

Listen

There are songs out there
that deliver my truths
in such a way
that maybe, in another's voice,
you might be able to finally
hear me

So, when I ask you to listen
to a song I've chosen,
there's a reason

Don't just hear the words,
listen –
and finally
hear **ME**

Après Vous

The ghosts
find their way,
no matter
the pace kept

Instead of
exhibiting fear,
I'll invite them
in for coffee

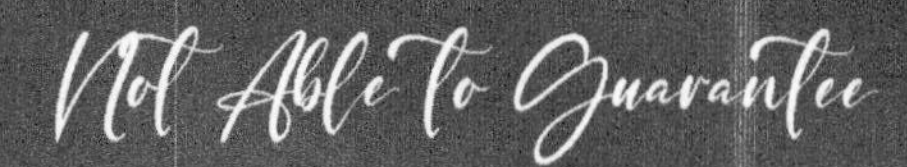

The night takes over,

not able to guarantee

safe space till morning

Divergence

You are on my mind
This seems to be my
w e a k n e s s
And, somehow
you are also my
STRENGTH

Scent of a Memory

It was the earliest of mornings,
where a mixture of scents
created a memory so real
it brought back the past of targets
and checks thrown together,
  waiting for them to be collected,
  praying it would be
  during a down time –
    70s music hummed low...
    a scent added in...
    cool water so intoxicating
    the mind turned
    and the heart woke
    from its deep slumber
But it was just a **memory**
swirled together by
scents of
coffee and white musk

I Withdraw

In one moment, I hear a love
professed so loud,
so strongly –

promises made
and now
promises silenced...

Do I mean so little
you still cling to a sparkle
without the actual thrill?

Are you oblivious to the one
full of enchantment,
the true magic
your short response
speaks for you?

I withdraw
without enough magic,
it seems,
to make you stay

Us

As long as there's a heart,
love will be flowing

As long as there is a soul,
the Divine essence will guide

As long as there's a mind,
ideas will keep coming

As long as there's a body,
strength will fight through

And as long as there is a **ME**,
there will always be a **YOU**

Thaumaturgie

Coming from a place
where magic wasn't allowed,
I found solace in these years gone by,
where now I was finally living
enchanted by activating that magic
in **e v e r y** place I could

Safe Now

Release this bound chaos

Walk away with my head held high

Trust I am safe now

Shifting Away

Vague recollections
are what I have left,
and it is in these moments
I find many questions

The truth of it all
is that you always held my soul,
and the feelings of regret
haunt my very being

Maybe I've moved on,
and it's possible you win,
because my heart is yours
even though I'm now g o n e

First Dance

The dance began
in a desperate way,
a clinging like no other,
  moving earth and sky
  with so much sanctified
  inside you

Justified,
I believed
I needed this connection

Even to this day,
I'm waiting in the wings
for one more chance
at that very first dance

This Time of Fear

Take this heart,
and place it around you

Though you feel torn apart,
together, we all stand true

Bless the lost
Bless the living

Hold each other near

My heart to you I'm giving

Sending support
in this time of fear

Creation

I am the magic
waving the wand I create –
It all starts with me

The Magic of Being Heard

There's magic in her step,
  a trail of glitter following
  with each step taken
She aims high to be one
with her celestial family
There's an enchanting flow
as she walks this earth
The grass and flowers
she walks with
bring brilliant understanding
to all the silence,
the hush of the starlit sky
as she captivates the stars
where she finds gratitude for release,
appreciating this audience

And finally,
as she hugs the trees
and is lit up by the moon,
she finds peace because
she was heard

Ghosts

Many stories are not all made up
Sometimes they are actually tangible
in the flesh,
and we have to cover them
so we can view them properly -

stories becoming more like ghosts
with each and every telling

Hope Signals

Pour your soul out
over the flowers
and send out hope signals
to the stars

Shadow Dance

My heart was born full -
  full of hope
  full of dreams
  full of wonder

As I grew older,
my heart was stomped on
and lied to,
thrown around and disregarded
In short,
  it was broken

Becoming an adult,
I took back my heart
I vowed to protect it,
  love it,
  cherish it

I survived
all of the shadow dances
and took my place
in the light
with my heart
safely in tow

Method of Breakage

They each had to go
right when happiness was found,
leaving me broken

The Illusionist

The moment I met you, I easily fell under your spell, and it was then I decided I'd allow myself to be happily tricked by all of your treats, because for the first time, I found someone who could tame my inner monsters.

This moment has passed. I stand in time, looking back. The abyss of us is quiet, buried in hours. We no longer reach each other. There is silence where there was pain.

Sometimes, the person who saves us becomes a poison. We drink it to die and be reborn.

But then we must *leave*.

Ode To Breakdown

In a room, all alone, she sits and wonders how she got to this point. Away from all that is familiar, stripped of all that is known and once thought to be needed, she lays down and closes her eyes.

Those voices that steered her too far off course.
The surrounding people did not understand.

She wants to be heard but is scared to yell. She had been bent so far that she crumbled. She broke down and was segregated in a world surrounded by the unknown. No other words to describe what was going on except that she was in the process of a complete breakdown.

Pushed to the limits, she comes to a realization...

It is okay to feel this way.
It is okay to feel lost at times.
It's okay to ask for help.
It's okay to say no.
It does not make a person less than a person. People are just not okay all of the time,
and that is **okay.**

Praying and lost in thought, she seeks and finds complete solace within herself. Stripped of all that she felt she had to have to keep going, she finds herself in the darkness and somehow finds clarity and sense from this pain.

She is ***surviving***.

Interruption of Peace

Constant fear grips me
paralyzed in many ways,
I'm uncomfortable

The pain I am in
is nothing I can describe
I'm ready to cry

Peace interrupted
Unfair chaos takes over –
chaos without love
Pain like no other
  disrupts all found peace,
  bequeaths a loss of all stillness

Anxiety runs
every aspect of this life

please just let me be

I Won't Give You Strength

Pain visits all these places,
lacking comfort and peace
Stopping medicine hurts -
it pulls me apart

Where I was still, I tremble
burning beneath the opiate dream
where cure becomes curse

Under moonlit skies,
secrets always bring stillness
resulting in regained peace

This constant struggle
results in a pendulum existence,
dragging me back and forth in its reality

Hearing all my cries,
not allowed to have a break,
I began to shut down

I will sit right here,
begging for any repose
Something has to give

The night takes over,
not able to guarantee
safe space till morning

Shutting it down,
this heart has become too broken

There will be no more
throwing caution out
Realizing my needs first
I cannot carry on this way

No longer afraid,
I deserve to walk right away -
entering a new life

Coming from a place
where I can create it
means becoming alive

The chances are high
I might, in fact, lose my mind
But I won't give you that strength

Facing it head on
in fields of paper flowers
I find true freedom

To find my safety,
realizing I can go on,
I keep safety here
  tucked inside me

Uncertainty

Reaching and watching these ins and outs,
I feel so inspired

But when it comes down to it,
I want to do more
than just **ADMIRE**

Fear takes control and chaos
e n s u e s
I don't feel I stack up as an equal next
to you

Even though there are so many things
I have mastered
At the heart of things,
I am a
beautiful disaster

Then, Here, Now

I have known myself
through others' sight, mind, and soul
It's time
to open my own eyes

to release these binding chains
and walk away with my head held high
Trust safety now

Given everything,
you're always a step ahead
Nothing's left in the past

I am the magic
waving my wand
I create,
and it all starts with me

Then - false energy
Here - I will take myself back
Now - the path is mine
Finally - ***I free myself***

Who? What? Where?

You started it,
or did I?
Years gone by
haven't changed
any of this mutual desire

Under your spell
is where I find myself,
and the longing is real,

but this is my new normal

Am I destined to be
this way going forward?
Is there a way out of
something I climbed into?
Do you know? Do you?

Even though I'm sinking fast,
I'll gladly drown in you –
even from afar

Unison

There's nothing more important,
more meaningful,
or more significant
than words I take in from you
The significance of your being,
your presence in my life,
is life-changing
I will always spend time
on you
with you
and for you
Your presence in this world
mirrors with my own
We are two sides of a
pearlescent shell
deep in the glittering ocean

Every Time

Come for me
Comfort me
Hold me,
and love me
Once you do,
expect me to be unconditional
Expect devotion and trust
with never ending love
If you accept these things,
then stay close,
because
I'll come for you
every time

Defiance

I'm in charge here, sir
You will find what you need here
My dress makes it so

My tiara means
I can create all I want here -

Don't Give Up on Me

I'm not just a thing...

I create windstorms of words
using the power of my mind

I won't be broken
In my smiling face are hints -
BEAUTY IN BREAKDOWNS

Dare I go to play
where all the magic resides,
surprised it's inside of me

It is possible
without grand gestures needed
Small things are created -
micro or macro

Surprises come from nowhere -
my superpower u n f o l d s

Under the oak tree,
there's a magical doorway,
a place I have made

Let me play a game
I am creating something
with these powers

It's time - come and join in
The magic crown allows it
Pure enchantment thrives,
allowing for rest

It stirs this creative energy
sounds so promising,
its muted chaos

Words seem to lose their meaning
Show me by actions

Far too many thoughts
gather at the wrong moments,
finding strength in madness

There aren't anymore -
the ones like all the others
left to pick the rest of me apart

Understanding this
is incomprehensible,
so don't give up on me

Fears take over time
which is not to be wasted
Please, release it all

Crying seems to help,
cleansing all impurities
I beg - *Take me home*

Unsure what to say,
thoughts riddle me like bullets
Peace is all I ask

Reaching out your way
only I'm to be ignored
Must I even try?

Ablaze

There was once cool water
beside a park
With a hint of white musk,
these scents combined
to create a home
surrounded by fragile union,
and little did he know,
every time he tried
to put out my fire

he actually set my
heart ablaze

Reassembling Love

There is nothing better than
to be dismantled by you
night
  after
    night
then put back together
morning
  after
    morning

Sanctified

Reaching cool waters,
I'm drowning in musk
I am **sanctified**

Let go
Just let go
Walk away with dignity
It's clear -*you aren't mine*

Mistakes can be made
Accidents can just happen
Release all the blame

Unravel and undo
Come undone
within the taste of your skin -
I give in

Encontró

On our journey,
we stand in a type
of independent camaraderie
We experience connectivity
while remaining independent
I see the familiar parts of you
in the seeking,
in the joy
and the wonder
There are whispers in the wind
guiding your every step
Even if you feel as though you might be lost,
you're always going the right way

Freed by Constancy

Sitting in complication,
I lean toward finding distraction,
and just like that,
the scent of days gone by
is recalled
with questions of why

No other person
can cause this reaction

It's not one of longing,
but rather, of appreciation

I now know my worth
I now know my heart
I now know my soul

All because
you never let go

One

Her stoic nature
made for a patient stance,
and even in the unknown,
she found comfort
Together,
divinity and she
walked hand in hand,
content,
and in so doing,
they became one
in perfect
peaceful
trust

Gratitude

She looked at
this woman before her
She thanked
her lucky stars
for every rough patch
she encountered
along the way
because it all led
to meeting her

Time's Up

I have found myself
in between all the pages
filled with words or blank

Let it all come out
you filthy excuse of man
Throw me to the wolves

I'll celebrate me
and inspiration now -
the stars are aligned

Thirty years later,
butterflies are still present
with every word you said

Time's up
I'm ready
You became my true happy -
no place - only heartfelt

Knowing how this ends
kills me every day
I just wanted to love

We both had to go
right when happiness was ours
leaving us **bro ken**

I Keep You Alive

Unlike any night,
I find myself missing you
and regretting the letting go
the lengths you went to
unnoticed and forgotten -
always my regret

I keep you alive...
word by word, thought by thought
You'd prefer me dead
You don't understand
I would have given you my all,
leading by my heart
No understanding
"Be a good girl and just smile"
Now - **the win is mine**

So misunderstood,
thrown in the limelight early,
losing pieces of myself

You fucking coward
Ten years
and it's thrown away...
all due to falseness
So much better off
losing a psychic vampire
It's time to let go

Better without you...
you broke all that was sacred
Don't try returning
You are no longer welcome
the worst kind of person -
a deceitful sheep

You ran and broke me
without so much as a call
You lost a good thing
You have made it clear -
zero respect, zero fucks
and you - a deceiver

I'll never forget
the way you lied to my face
and tore it all down
I see your true colors
You're not who you claim to be
Now I question it all

Nothing was ever
gained as a result of years
of lies and false hopes

In you, I can see
a traitor, a false profit
despite claims of Godliness -
deception with words,
absence of truth,
lies in all you said

My brave has found me,
not in the absence of fear
but in spite of it

Love is all about
forgiving past mistakes
and moving forward

Thank God you are gone
You always pushed my limits
You didn't care

In a place and time
where your words are meaningless,
PLEASE, NEVER COME BACK

To become the best version of yourself is about learning to love the worst version too. Forgiving, moving forward, letting go, learning not everything is about you. Realizing you can't control others, but you can control your reactions.

Light

Sometimes the situation
calls for seeing the truth
at any cost,
and so many insist
that it's morally gray
or that it's black not white

What if we see things
from a more positive
point of view?

Gazing at situations
and finding the light
can give such a
different perspective

Go to the light,
and watch your
attitude change

Learn

All are your
best friends
All are your
teachers

Life is about
keeping the
good times close
and the less than
perfect times...***closer***

My Before and After*

Otherworldly experiences...
 a past that is painful -
This is my before

Emotions ran high,
 pain, fear, sadness
a broken soul,
coming to the conclusion
I had to break the cycle

I stood up
I broke the mold
My afterwards became
so bright and inspirational -
the ability to stride
into a life that was my own,
the strength it took

I had to find my bravery,
and I did

I really did that

Bring Me at Night, One Star*

I feel your presence in the scent of cool waters,
and the white musk that showed me peace
The sun guides me, shines a light on me,
reminds me that I have a very good life
The words exchanged are truly enough

I don't ask for much
I don't need much
I don't even want much

But still, in the midnight hour
I look out my window,
and I find your soul entwined with mine
The moon seems to wink at me,
as I am thankful I am here in the dark

Bring me at night, one star - just one
that lets me know you think of me too

Bad Timing

This wasn't the time to ask for more,
but I needed this moment to go on
The words you would string together
might help make sense of each epitome I came to
It never occurred to me just how
gorgeous this process was
or how to properly express my
lasting appreciation

Coast down the shoreline,
scenes of blue buckets by day
and dark black by night

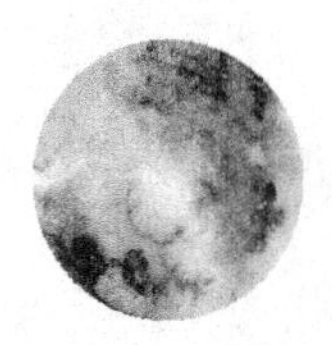

Unbolted the Door to Two Moons*

locked inside
brings fear
unbolted doors to two moons
finding the bright light

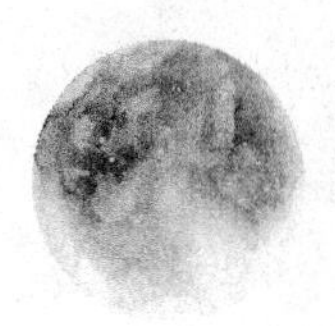

*Eager for the Undergrowth**

So much has held me back
from the child struck down again and again
to the young adult trapped in a situation
that I could not possibly get out of

Deciding to take back my life one day
created a deep sense of eagerness
to grow not only on the surface
but to dig deep and allow the darkness
to be a gift as well as the light

and the undergrowth is the root
propelling me upward for greatness

To Make It*

I was privy early on
to the truth surrounding me
in such a way that I knew,
in order to secure any sort of future,
I would have to work twice as hard
just to make it
But I believed I could,
and now I look around my life,
and not only did I just make it,
I own the whole damn world

*Daily in a Tiny Upstairs Room**

Daily in tiny
upstairs room with no escape,
IT'S TIME TO BREAK FREE

a little patch of
somebody around would feel
like a thousand suns*

A Pile of If *

Life can be so messy
with lines crossed daily
For so long,
I believed
if **this** happened
then **that** would happen
It became almost a running joke
because there was unwillingness
to commit to actual change

I've come to the conclusion
I don't need a pile of IF
I deserve a pile of **WHEN**

*Let Water Chase**

Trusting in the flow
and living in the present
let water chase dreams

Stayed in a Hug*

Some days, there is too much anxiety,
and peace is nowhere in sight
Overwhelming feelings take over
But then that one person, my person,
wraps me up, and we stay in a hug,
and suddenly everything makes sense again

Divided Picnic Bread*

There are no more reasons
that I can come up with
to justify why I seem to need you
I am baffled by how much I care,
but you made it clear from day one
we would not go out into the world
as a unit
Staying in our own lane
was what you always wanted
After all I gave to you, all I shared,
you still sat down,
and divided even picnic bread

*In Her Own Kind**

Losing grip quickly,
safety meant
wrapping herself
in peace -
her own kind

Be With*

I need to understand
why you can't be with me now
Instead, you're away

Cadence

You're easily the single most
frustrating source in my life,
and though you don't
come right out and say it,
I am left questioning my
worth every time we talk

That's not you,
that's me, and I know it
I feel I am always two
steps behind you

Who said you had to be
the one to set the pace?

I Am

I am an earthquake.
a star child waiting to glow

I WILL NOT DARE STOP

Face Fully Close*

Lean in and breathe out,
and with my face fully close,
pull me into a kiss

Whole

Within all of life,
determined to create love,
I found you... my person

Understanding love
means accepting you as all
I'm here **forever,**

standing tall and straight
Stillness and peace are found
like preciousness of ice

Finding peace within
periods of gestation
pours hope into self,

joining forces within,
understanding divinity,
a bravely formed union,

focused awareness,
partnership with higher self
bringing togetherness

Newness will be formed
Look within at your higher self
Bonds of truths are found

Breathing in and out,
release thoughts of low self-worth
Divine union is found once more

Letting Go

Finding paths
to opening oneself up to the unknown,
to discovering the intricate nature of ins and outs,
the hows and the whys and the whats and the whos

A cryptic dream infused with images rushing by
brings hints of desires from past times, and now
focused discussion brings back these memories

It's a race to save them before their final goodbye

Blue Velvet Heart

Blue velvet heart
sealed in your glue

I never knew what it could be like
till you severed its hold
Who will I get in the morning
Who will I get tonight?

Blue velvet heart
severed of its glue

As a Poet

As a poet,
I find new ways
of looking at everything,
and I find my heart
expressed exponentially

As a poet,
I learn more about myself
while discovering
the chance to truly
express myself truthfully

As a poet,
I release thoughts
about people who don't
deserve to hear my voice,
and I am able to move on

Light and Dark

In the midst of hope and despair,
I relate more to the middle ground
The beauty of the light side
mixed with the darker aspects
allows me the means to appreciate
all aspects of myself -

the side that shines brighter than the stars
and the other side as black as night

The Ones I Keep Near

Dear You,
Do you know what these years have done to me?
Without hesitation, I can tell you
that you inspire me more than you will ever know,
and your hold on me
might have been loosened,
but the means in which you entered my realm
is never forgotten
The cool waters met the musky scents of rain,
and in that moment, I was lost in your eyes
I forgot how to live without you
I discovered new ways of thinking
I really had no idea what I was doing,
but you did
You flaunted others around me
You chose friends over me
You were around only when it was right for you
Did you not know how much you meant to me?
Or maybe you did,
and that is the reason for the absences
created over the years
All this to say...
you will never understand the workings of my heart
You won't know how you inspired me
every second of every day
Truly, I am thankful for the red moments
and the tan moments,
and I rest in the comfort of knowing
you keep your gaze short-sighted
while I focus mine
on the ones I keep close

Red Light

The gaze told the story
Childlike wonder was at play
Sometimes, even the arrows pointing right
meant the wrong direction
Struggling to find a reason
to understand what was conveyed,
even in the best of circumstances,
a red light stopped us all
The tiniest details
drove anxious thoughts
until an outsider spoke
There was no calm around

Breathe in:
one
two
three

My upper hand ushers in relief

Replenish

It's coming from all sides,
and I don't know how to say that I need a break
The ends aren't coming together,
and I am not sure how it even began

But, when I am with you, all the pieces
seem to fall into place, and these hands
instinctively long to reach for yours

Go ahead and tell me you need me,
and let me feel the calm I'm entitled to feel
Stepping away from the mirror,
I allow trust to restore
itself in my heart and my mind,
and once again, I believe I can do this

Mercury Rising

Life often leaves me tangled
I become all I didn't know -
unrecognizable, lost in mercury

Sometimes, it's the sheer glory,
awe, and flying high
Other times it's insecurity,
clenched fists, and preparing for the worst
But it's always worth it
The moments of victory must
be mixed with the shadows

All of it is ***a blessing***

Balance

I don't feel like disappointing you,
but I need to take this time away
With all of the ups and downs we face,
it can feel this is heading toward damage
I just need a place to stretch out,
a soft spot for my head to rest on
Listening to myself and my needs
doesn't mean I love you any less

I just love me more

Secret Weapon

Magic runs through me
by way of my words,
my thoughts,
my feelings,
and my actions

The gorgeous beauty
that is the result
causes me to live in awe daily
Not only
do those around me benefit,
but I become
my own secret weapon

Beauty in the Breakdown

There are some things you should know about me
I am proud of who I am,
especially when you know *who I've been*
I promise I will take up space,
because I haven't been allowed before
I've been through a lot and felt so much,
but I will do the work to come out on top
The world I live in is a world I've made mine,
because it was never my own for years
I see beauty in the essence of daily life,
and I see it in the deep recesses of my heart
as well as in the mirror in front of me
My environment is one I have created,
and it is whole and **full of promise**
I found that, rather that meandering about in fear,
I walk with confidence and trust,
not only in the world I have built from scratch,
but I've learned I can trust myself
And after knowing this,
I can take on any challenge that comes my way
I have found ***beauty*** in the **breakdown**

The Pink Cottage

What wonderful peace I have found
in the loving arms of quiet solace
It's in the retreat that I have calmed down,
and this is how I hear her

What a life changer this solitude is,
bringing me light in places once too dark,
not knowing how I lived like this
Such is the need for deep reflection

The pink cottage down the path
is where I can go to find time away,
and the silence brings thoughts to catch
This is a luxury I find myself enjoying

Stillness is often the journey itself,
just to find time alone in this chaos,
feeling the hermit's energy and help
Spirit pulls me into her blanket of peace

This is the light in the dark I've needed
This is the quiet and the silence
This is the answer to why I retreated
This is the reason for spiritual solitude

Cease

There's no holding back,
can't hold it in any more
You have crossed
ALL
my lines.

Spell

The gloom of a soul
often creates the flame
of another one

One Door Closes

There are some goodbyes
that are disguised as
another chance

Another Door Opens

Wholeness

Darkness tells stories
while light speaks
of the triumphs,
and both sides
connect

Shine

I am allowing myself to
be cracked open,
and I am willing to explore
what comes out
I will fight the fear I feel
when I come across some
things in my way

This is my chance to shine

Acknowledgments

There are so many people I want to acknowledge, I couldn't possibly list them all, but there are a few that need to be mentioned.

To my loving other half, Zach, I don't know what I would do without your love and support and encouragement to keep writing and to keep moving ahead. For that, I am forever thankful. You handle my moods, my ups and downs, and my inside outs so effortlessly and I am so blessed to have you by my side. I know you are always going to be there.

To my son, Austin - what can I say? You are undoubtedly my greatest gift in this life. I want you to know that I am grateful for every time you are there, whether it be to remind me to take my medicine or to help me when I don't feel well or making me chicken nuggets when I forget to eat. Knowing you are here is a tremendous comfort.

To Chris (& Terry), thank you for being my family, for being there at any and all times I need you. Thank you for going out of your way to help me, especially during the major transition period 20 years ago. Because of you, I am the person I am today, because of you I was allowed opportunities that I wouldn't have had otherwise and because of you, I know what true, unconditional love is. Because of you, I'm no longer alone, or afraid.

To Candice, Ashley and Angie, I could not have created this book without each of you. You all believed in me and gave me encouragement when I was feeling not so great about moving forward. The messages we share daily keep me going in the right direction. I am so grateful for the love, support and guidance each of you bring, to not only my writing, but my life as a whole. Each of you are so beautiful inside and out, so talented and so loving. I count myself so lucky to have you all in my life.

To Betty, your guidance and love have changed my life. I was in a completely different head space when I met you, and through your advice I have transformed my entire life. Your mentoring and the way you always steer me in the right direction is invaluable and I am forever grateful we met.

To Luann, what would I do without you? Your way of showing me love and support is something I have not known in a friendship in a very long time. We just connect and get each other in a way that makes my heart sing. Thank you for everything you have done for me and in the time we have known each other, I have become a better person.

To Lori, you are amazing. From helping me keep my house running to getting me out of the house to taking me to run errands, you are an invaluable friend and I am so very blessed to have you in my life. You have helped me in ways I cannot possibly express and you have given me a sense of independence when I am often stuck at home. I have a more well-rounded and enriched life because of you.

To Hope, Beth and Lisa, I would be lost without our daily talks, our letters we send back and forth and your general facilitation of guidance and advice which have made my whole world a better place. To know I can always count on each of you when I need to talk, receive advice or participate in writing prompts together - all of it makes a difference and all of it is well appreciated.

To Mandy, thank you for your prompts when I needed them, thank you for introducing me to the Hope Beacon and thank you for your continued help in guiding me. I am so thankful for you and how you have a way with inspiring words out of my soul when I feel stuck.

To Kari, my sister, thank you for your love you've shown me for over 2 decades. You are a rare person who can light up my life with a single word and you are one of the only people whom I cannot talk to for days, but pick right back up where we left off. You are a blessing to me. Thank you.

To Lara and Diana, thank you for support from the get go. You have helped me grow as a poet and it is a true honor to be featured on your site monthly. And Diana, thank you for helping me get my poetry ready for sharing and for your nurturing nature.

To Tiffany, your love for me and your gentle prodding have continuously led me into a growth mindset. Your way of seeing into my heart and mind and knowing what I need at the right time. Having you on my side, as my guide as well as my cheerleader, has been invaluable in my life and I'm definitely improving one day at a time because of you.

To Peni and Willie's Women, I have immense gratitude for the support and compassion you give. And for allowing me a platform to share my gifts and talents. I consider it a blessing to have a place I belong.

And finally, those who know me, know my love for Jeremy Renner, Elizabeth Mitchell and Amy Lee - their movies, music and television shows have been there for me when I have felt lost, anxious or sad and have even helped lessen the pain I feel daily. I just had to include this last little bit because, as silly as it sounds, I am happier because of these people.

About the Author

Renee Lynn Furlow lives in Texas with her son and husband and two gorgeous cats. Renee began writing as early as four years of age, it came naturally to her, but it's also been her medicine. She recognizes that for her at least, reading and writing are a necessary balm through challenging times, and a super-power when you need to believe in yourself and keep going.

Renee regularly wrote for several newspapers and was actively engaged in the writing community from a young age, both at High School and afterwards. She is a huge supporter of literacy and the power of reading, not least to defeat hardships and give yourself more chances in life and grow as a person. Since 2010 Renee has regularly written for various online sites. She also ran her own site, 'Magic Musperations' where she featured other's writings. This, her first solo book of poetry, is the culmination of many years of writing, including her regular spot with Kind Over Matter, each month for over a decade.

Renee has battled with her fair share of severe chronic illnesses in her young life so far. At times it has been overwhelming to try to carve out a life with so many serious illnesses trying to hold her back. Luckily, Renee is a born survivor. She didn't get this far to quit now, and even on the hard days, she's reminded of how many believe in her, and hold her up, even when it seems insurmountable. That strength and courage is inbuilt in Renee since she was a little girl, having to get past things that no child should endure. Not every day is easy, but Renee's mantra is to thrive rather than merely exist. For those who understand the unique challenges of living with multiple-chronic-illnesses, you'll be familiar with how this isn't easy. Giving up is not Renee's personality, she's a fighter, and a lover, and those strengths come into play in her writing and how she selflessly gives back to others.

The core takeaway from Renee's struggles is her willingness to love and find joy in little things, which keeps her going even when she's in the hospital. When her friends compliment her on her strength, she reminds them that they play a big part in how she gets through the toughest challenges. Writing and reading have always helped Renee's imagination soar above the pains of the everyday and remind her of her potential and enduring dreams.

Renee's work has been featured in 8 anthologies including SMITTEN This Is What Love Looks Like by Indie Blu(e) Publishing (being honored as a National Indie Excellence Award Finalist) and Glow, Self Care Poetry for the Soul by Indie Earth Publishing.

If you summed up Renee's life so far it might include avid reader, mother, wife, friend, creative writer, poet, witchy, gothic woman who never gives up.

Candice Louisa Daquin
Psychotherapist NBCC/LPC/LADC/SAACT/SAC/D-SAACP
Tainted by the Same Counterfeit - Finishing Line Press, 2022

Made in the USA
Coppell, TX
09 November 2023

23948180R00066